Smart Riddles For Smart Kids

*400 Interactive Riddles & Trick Questions
For Kids And Family*

DINGO
BOOK CLUB

"Great Books Change Life"

Table of Contents

INTRODUCTION 15

RIDDLES 1 TO 100 16

    QUESTION #1: WHOSE SON? 16
    QUESTION #2: TIME RIDER 16
    QUESTION #3: NOT AS MANY AS YOU THINK 16
    QUESTION #4: KIDS OF ALL SHAPES AND SIZES 16
    QUESTION #5: JUST DO IT 16
    QUESTION #6: IT'S ALL IN YOUR HEAD 17
    QUESTION #7: INTERNATIONAL CABIN 17
    QUESTION #8: A LITERAL BET 17
    QUESTION #9: AS YOU WERE WALKING 17
    QUESTION #10: MUSICAL STRAWBERRIES 17
    QUESTION #11: WALK THIS WAY 18
    QUESTION #12: YOUR WELL.. 18
    QUESTION #13: THINGS AREN'T AS TALL AS THEY SEEM........ 18
    QUESTION #14: LEGAL VIOLATION 18
    QUESTION #15: BREAKING THE PATTERN 18
    QUESTION #16: A COAT OF COLORS 19
    QUESTION #17: UNFASHIONABLE DRESS............................ 19
    QUESTION #18: VIOLENT RING....................................... 19
    QUESTION #19: SUPER MARIO'S ROOM 19
    QUESTION #20: WE ARE FAMILY....................................... 19
    QUESTION #21: COCKIEST OF THEM ALL 20
    QUESTION #22: WOOD IN THE WIND................................ 20
    QUESTION #23: FAST AND FURIOUS 20
    QUESTION #24: THE LOVE BOAT 20
    QUESTION #25: FIT TO A T 20
    QUESTION #26: IT'S NOT WHAT YOU THINK IT IS 21
    QUESTION #27: IT STAYS WITH YOU.................................. 21
    QUESTION #28: PANTS-LESS BARNES AND NOBLE 21
    QUESTION #29: HEAVYWEIGHT CHAMPION OF THE WORLD....... 21
    QUESTION #30: NEWTON'S FOOTBALL 21
    QUESTION #31: COOL AS ICE... 22
    QUESTION #32: FIXED SHADES... 22

QUESTION #33: THE STRANGE CASE OF DEXTER BUTTON 22
QUESTION #34: REAL STEEL.. 22
QUESTION #35: WET IF YOU DO, WET IF YOU DON'T 22
QUESTION #36: A HARMLESS STALKER 23
QUESTION #37: ALL BOXED IN 23
QUESTION #38: A DIFFERENT KIND OF MATH 23
QUESTION #39: JUST BETWEEN THE TWO OF US 23
QUESTION #40: YOU CAN'T WET SOMETHING THAT'S.. 23
QUESTION #41: HONORABLE COVETING 24
QUESTION #42: OLAF... 24
QUESTION #43: EVERYBODY'S HERE 24
QUESTION #44: IT'S HOW YOU READ IT 24
QUESTION #45: AIR BALL.. 24
QUESTION #46: THE STRANGE CASE OF BENJAMIN BUTTON.................................. 25
QUESTION #47: COMBUSTIBLE STICK... 25
QUESTION #48: LUCKY 1,000.. 25
QUESTION #49: A BAT YOU ARE NOT 25
QUESTION #50: AUTOBOTS...ROLL OUT 25
QUESTION #51: PIRATED COINS 26
QUESTION #52: LONG LOST FRIENDS... 26
QUESTION #53: ENGLISH MATES 26
QUESTION #54: ROUND AND ROUND THE FAMILY GOES 26
QUESTION #55: TEA DAYS.. 26
QUESTION #56: NOT AS MANY AS YOU THINK 27
QUESTION #57: TICKLES COUNTDOWN 27
QUESTION #58: SAME AS YOURS 27
QUESTION #59: THE ANSWER'S HERE... 27
QUESTION #60: IT'S A NUMBERS GAME... 27
QUESTION #61: WHO'S THE FAIREST OF US ALL?... 28
QUESTION #62: THERE'S A LOT OF IT HERE.. 28
QUESTION #63: NOT MEANT TO BE BROKEN... 28
QUESTION #64: PUNGENCY REQUIRED 28
QUESTION #65: CRYING HIGH IN THE SKY.. 28
QUESTION #66: POWER YOU UP 29
QUESTION #67: ALSO A GUMMY TREAT... 29
QUESTION #68: AN EQUIPMENT... 29
QUESTION #69: I RAISE YOU UP 29
QUESTION #70: EVIDENCE OF APPROVAL 29

4

QUESTION #71: I WON'T TELL IT TO YOU..30
QUESTION #72: NOT SO HIGH..30
QUESTION #73: AN UNWELCOMED GUEST THAT PEOPLE RUN OVER..........................30
QUESTION #74: SWEET DREAMS..30
QUESTION #75: ROUND AND ROUND IT GOES...30
QUESTION #76: FAMILY TIES..31
QUESTION #77: COLORS ON THE ROAD..31
QUESTION #78: COMMAND CENTER...31
QUESTION #79: PICTURES PAINT A THOUSAND WORDS...31
QUESTION #80: DIRECTIONS...31
QUESTION #81: MAKING MELODIES...32
QUESTION #82: IT'S HIGH AND HOT..32
QUESTION #83: THE CORRECT INCORRECT ANSWER...32
QUESTION #84: RECORDS TRANSACTIONS...32
QUESTION #85: UNDER THE SEA...32
QUESTION #86: A SHELTER..33
QUESTION #87: YOU WRITE ON IT..33
QUESTION #88: I HELP YOU WRITE...33
QUESTION #89: THE UN-CAT...33
QUESTION #90: WISDOM IN WORDS..33
QUESTION #91: BURN BABY BURN, BURN!..34
QUESTION #92: YOU, ME, AND JESSE DUPREE...34
QUESTION #93: IT'S A CORRUPT BULL..34
QUESTION #94: THE ROOT DETERMINES THE FRUIT..34
QUESTION #95: SMOKE IN YOUR MIND...34
QUESTION #96: TRUE OR FALSE?...35
QUESTION #97: A WHITE FLOWER...35
QUESTION #98: DO AS YOU'RE TOLD..35
QUESTION #99: COMMANDER IN CHIEF...35
QUESTION #100: ALADDIN'S MAGIC RIDE...35

RIDDLES 101 TO 200 36

QUESTION #101: LEAN ON ME..36
QUESTION #102: THE CIRCLES OF LIFE..36
QUESTION #103: NEWLINE CINEMA..36
QUESTION #104: APPLES...TRANSFORMED!...36
QUESTION #105: SUBTRACTION...36
QUESTION #106: DEEPER INSIDE...37

5

QUESTION #107: A LIBRARIAN'S FAVORITE WORD.................................... 37
QUESTION #108: LINE AND SINKER 37
QUESTION #109: EXPECT THE UNEXPECTED.. 37
QUESTION #110: NOT AS FAR AS YOU THINK 37
QUESTION #111: THE REAL KING OF THE ANIMALS 38
QUESTION #112: PAY ATTENTION 38
QUESTION #113: IT'S JUST A FANTASY... 38
QUESTION #114: CHRISTMAS BALLS.. 38
QUESTION #115: CHECKMATE! 38
QUESTION #116: DUAL ROLE... 39
QUESTION #117: THE DEVIL'S IN THE DETAILS 39
QUESTION #118: STAIRWAY TO WHERE? 39
QUESTION #119: IT'S SO SOFT 39
QUESTION #120: SO MANY BARS... 39
QUESTION #121: HAND READING 40
QUESTION #122: A LETTER.. 40
QUESTION #123: IT RINGS A BELL 40
QUESTION #124: THE BEST MOVIE COMPANION...................................... 40
QUESTION #125: GONE WITH IT 40
QUESTION #126: LET THERE BE... 41
QUESTION #127: BORROWED BUT NOT LENT 41
QUESTION #128: YOU LOSE TRACK OF IT MANY TIMES............................... 41
QUESTION #129: SMALL BUT POWERFUL.. 41
QUESTION #130: LIKE A POPSICLE 41
QUESTION #131: YOU PROVIDE IT THE HEAD AND ARMS 42
QUESTION #132: SHINES SO BRIGHT.. 42
QUESTION #133: DON'T PLAY WITH IT.. 42
QUESTION #134: MAKES YOU LOOK GOOD.. 42
QUESTION #135: FILLED WITH SAND 42
QUESTION #136: A MEASURING DEVICE... 43
QUESTION #137: YOU WEAR IT 43
QUESTION #138: GIVES YOU SAP 43
QUESTION #139: YOU BUY WITH IT.. 43
QUESTION #140: THE LONE RANGER 43
QUESTION #141: NIKES, ADIDAS, AND UNDERARMOUR 44
QUESTION #142: IT CAN ALSO BE A SOUP.. 44
QUESTION #143: CREAMY AND CRISPY IT CAN BE.................................... 44
QUESTION #144: A HALLOWEEN FIXTURE 44

QUESTION #145: IT HAS FLIGHTS BUT NOT AN AIRPORT...44
QUESTION #146: PROTECTS FROM INTRUDERS 45
QUESTION #147: FLOWING LIKE A RIVER 45
QUESTION #148: OUT OF THE HEART THE MOUTH DOES 45
QUESTION #149: BUGS BUNNY'S FAVORITE TREAT...45
QUESTION #150: PIERCES SHARPLY 45
QUESTION #151: A KIND OF STONE..46
QUESTION #152: IT CONTAINS LIQUIDS...46
QUESTION #153: MAKE BREAD FROM IT 46
QUESTION #154: A JOKE THAT ISN'T FUNNY 46
QUESTION #155: IT CAN BE SCRAMBLED 46
QUESTION #156: IT WAS HIDDEN UNDER A PRINCESS' MATTRESS 47
QUESTION #157: SEE WITH IT...47
QUESTION #158: HARDLY PRESENT 47
QUESTION #159: ALWAYS ON THE HORIZON 47
QUESTION #160: AQUAMAN'S SPECIALTY 47
QUESTION #161: A PLURAL WORD 48
QUESTION #162: NOT A DRUG 48
QUESTION #163: SURPRISING..48
QUESTION #164: CLASSIC VOLKSWAGEN CAR..48
QUESTION #165: COLE HAANS, HUSH PUPPIES...48
QUESTION #166: A TOTALLY BLACK ELEPHANT 49
QUESTION #167: JOAQUIN PHOENIX' SIBLING 49
QUESTION #168: PART OF A CONVENIENCE STORE'S NAME 49
QUESTION #169: IT CAN BE GREEN AND HOT AND COMES IN A BAG 49
QUESTION #170: UP, UP AND AWAY ON MY BEAUTIFUL...49
QUESTION #171: A UNIT OF MEASURE (WEIGHT)...50
QUESTION #172: IT'S ALL IN YOUR MIND 50
QUESTION #173: IT'S A BIRD THAT'S NOT A BIRD...50
QUESTION #174: KIDS IN PRESCHOOL SING THIS...50
QUESTION #175: DUMBO IS BEST KNOWN FOR THIS 50
QUESTION #176: FULL OR HALF MAST IT STANDS 51
QUESTION #177: IT'S A CREEPY CRAWLY 51
QUESTION #178: YOU CAN HYPNOTIZE WITH IT 51
QUESTION #179: WHITE AND YELLOW IS IT'S THEME..51
QUESTION #180: IT'S A PART OF YOUR MIND...51
QUESTION #181: EAT WITH IT...52
QUESTION #182: IT'S ALSO THE NAME OF COURTNEY LOVE'S BAND 52

7

QUESTION #183: IT'S IN YOUR HANDS 52
QUESTION #184: IT'S HALF-MEANT... 52
QUESTION #185: YOU SLEEP WITH IT.. 52
QUESTION #186: IT'S NOT HOT 53
QUESTION #187: SLIPPERY WHEN WET... 53
QUESTION #188: IT'S A DAILY THING 53
QUESTION #189: IT'S WOOD YOU CAN BLOW 53
QUESTION #190: A BIG, BAD WOLF LOVES THIS 53
QUESTION #191: A HEALTHY FOOD 54
QUESTION #192: SOUNDS LIKE AN ENERGIZED ADMIRER 54
QUESTION #193: EVERYBODY IS PRESENT 54
QUESTION #194: ROLL CALL - DONE!... 54
QUESTION #195: SOMETHING CHEAP... 54
QUESTION #196: SUPPLY AND DEMAND.. 55
QUESTION #197: HAIL CAESAR NUMBERS 55
QUESTION #198: ALL OR NOTHING.. 55
QUESTION #199: IT'S A STATE.. 55
QUESTION #200: THE LOVE MONTH 55

RIDDLES 201 TO 300 ....**56**

QUESTION #201: IT'S A MATTER OF GEOGRAPHY 56
QUESTION #202: PLAY ON WORDS 56
QUESTION #203: NBA TEAMS, ONE EAST AND ONE WEST 56
QUESTION #204: FAMILY TIES... 56
QUESTION #205: COUNT IT RIGHT... 56
QUESTION #206: RAVENS ARE SENSIBLE CREATURES.. 57
QUESTION #207: FLYING ON A STRING 57
QUESTION #208: IT'S THE GENDER... 57
QUESTION #209: IN AND OUT AND FINAL COUNT 57
QUESTION #210: REVERSE PSYCHOLOGY.. 57
QUESTION #211: FROM UNDER THE SEA TO OUT OF IT 58
QUESTION #212: IT'S MADE OF PAPER 58
QUESTION #213: THE SIDE OF EVIL.. 58
QUESTION #214: IT'S ALL ABOUT YOU 58
QUESTION #215: OKLAHOMA CITY SPORTS TEAM 58
QUESTION #216: YOU PLAY WITH THEM 59
QUESTION #217: SKY STREAKERS 59
QUESTION #218: RESTING IN PEACE 59

8

QUESTION #219: AN ORAL EXPERT 59
QUESTION #220: IT MAKES THE WORLD A HEALTHIER PLACE TO LIVE 59
QUESTION #221: A COLLECTORS' ITEM 60
QUESTION #222: A HERO IN A HALF SHELL 60
QUESTION #223: IT'S POSSIBLE 60
QUESTION #224: YOU LIGHT IT UP 60
QUESTION #225: CROSSING A RIVER 60
QUESTION #226: GEOGRAPHY MATTERS 61
QUESTION #227: TWO'S COMPANY, THREE'S A CROWD 61
QUESTION #228: DO THE MATH 61
QUESTION #229: LITERALLY 61
QUESTION #230: UNOFFICIAL DAYS 61
QUESTION #231: IT'S A NUMBERS GAME 62
QUESTION #232: LAYS GOLDEN EGGS 62
QUESTION #233: HONK-LESS ANIMALS 62
QUESTION #234: A SHY ANIMAL 62
QUESTION #235: IT'S A LETTER 62
QUESTION #236: THE OBVIOUS 63
QUESTION #237: THE CITY THAT HARDLY SLEEPS 63
QUESTION #238: CREATURES 63
QUESTION #239: THE MOST OBVIOUS ANSWERS 63
QUESTION #240: A GOVERNMENT INSTITUTION 63
QUESTION #241: IT'S NOT AN ACTUAL BODY PART 64
QUESTION #242: JURASSIC WORLD 64
QUESTION #243: IT'S A SONG BY RIHANNA 64
QUESTION #244: NOT X-RAY VISION 64
QUESTION #245: IT'S A LETTER 64
QUESTION #246: NO NEED TO DIG 65
QUESTION #247: IT'S A REAL CHEESE 65
QUESTION #248: YOU CAN SING IN IT 65
QUESTION #249: IT'S A DAY! 65
QUESTION #250: LOCATIONS 65
QUESTION #251: DUAL USE 66
QUESTION #252: PAY CLOSE ATTENTION TO READING 66
QUESTION #253: ON THE BEACH 66
QUESTION #254: A VERY EASY HUNT 66
QUESTION #255: ASIDE FROM A WET BEAR 66
QUESTION #256: IT'S ANNOYING 67

QUESTION #257: IT'S A MATTER OF PRONUNCIATION 67
QUESTION #258: NOT A REAL SHIP.. 67
QUESTION #259: IT'S A CONTAINER 67
QUESTION #260: SQUARE PANTS 67
QUESTION #261: SHE PLAYED A ROLE IN THE BEAUTY AND THE BEAST 68
QUESTION #262: HYDROPHOBIC ROCKS... 68
QUESTION #263: YOU CAN'T STOP IT FROM GOING UP.. 68
QUESTION #264: IT'S A FOOD 68
QUESTION #265: FOOD RELATED 68
QUESTION #266: IT HURTS... 69
QUESTION #267: NO NEED FOR DEEP THINKING HERE 69
QUESTION #268: YOU CAN PLAY WITH IT... 69
QUESTION #269: IT'S A WET BED 69
QUESTION #270: A LIONEL RICHIE CLASSIC HIT.. 69
QUESTION #271: MUTANT?.. 70
QUESTION #272: WAITING FOR YOUR TURN 70
QUESTION #273: A BODY PART 70
QUESTION #274: A 5-LETTER WORD 70
QUESTION #275: IT'S ALWAYS BEING SET DURING MEALS 70
QUESTION #276: YOUNGSTERS 71
QUESTION #277: SIT ON IT 71
QUESTION #278: HOLLYWOOD HAS LOTS OF THEM 71
QUESTION #279: IT'S REPETITIVE 71
QUESTION #280: YOU PICK IT UP OFTEN 71
QUESTION #281: IT RINGS BUT ISN'T A PHONE.. 72
QUESTION #282: YOU PLAY IT 72
QUESTION #283: IT CAN COME FROM A DOG BUT DOESN'T 72
QUESTION #284: PEOPLE OF THE SEA CAN DO IT.. 72
QUESTION #285: A SONG BY RIHANNA.. 72
QUESTION #286: IT MAKES UP MOST OF THE EARTH'S SURFACE.............................. 73
QUESTION #287: A GOO GOO DOLLS HIT SONG 73
QUESTION #288: HASSLE-FREE AND CHEAP.. 73
QUESTION #289: HOWEVER YOU LOOK AT THEM... 73
QUESTION #290: IT'S NAMED PARTIALLY AFTER THEM 73
QUESTION #291: ESPECIALLY AT THE BEACH... 74
QUESTION #292: A POPULAR SONG BY THE BEATLES... 74
QUESTION #293: IT'S OFTEN GREEN AND LEAFY... 74
QUESTION #294: THE ANSWER'S HERE.. 74

QUESTION #295: THE MOST OBVIOUS ANSWER IS THE ANSWER................................74
QUESTION #296: IT FLOWS 75
QUESTION #297: IT'S ALL ABOUT DISTANCE AND FUR 75
QUESTION #298: YOU GIVE HI-FIVES WITH IT...75
QUESTION #299: IT'S FAST, REALLY FAST...75
QUESTION #300: IT'S NOT AN OFFICIAL LANGUAGE 75

RIDDLES 301 TO 400 .... **76**

QUESTION #301: IT'S ALL ABOUT WATCHES 76
QUESTION #302: IT'S STILL ABOUT WATCHES...76
QUESTION #303: DO THE MATH 76
QUESTION #304: NO NEED TO DO THE MATH 76
QUESTION #305: IT'S A LUCKY NUMBER 76
QUESTION #306: IT'S ALIVE! 77
QUESTION #307: IT'S HEAVY 77
QUESTION #308: YOU SING IT IN PRESCHOOL...77
QUESTION #309: IT'S A DAIRY PRODUCT 77
QUESTION #310: IT'S A VERY CLUB-ISH SPORT..77
QUESTION #311: YOU COVER YOURSELF WITH IT TOO...78
QUESTION #312: IT'S PART OF THE RICE COOKER 78
QUESTION #313: A STATIONARY TRAVELER...78
QUESTION #314: YOU CAN EAT THIS CUP 78
QUESTION #315: A HALLOWEEN STAPLE 78
QUESTION #316: IT USUALLY STINKS 79
QUESTION #317: MICHAEL PHELPS 79
QUESTION #318: THE ANSWER'S OBVIOUS 79
QUESTION #319: YOU SEAL IT BEFORE SENDING 79
QUESTION #320: IT'S ABOUT THE BREAD..79
QUESTION #321: IF YOU READ CAREFULLY..80
QUESTION #322: IT'S A HOLLOW WORD 80
QUESTION #323: ANOTHER OBVIOUS ANSWER...80
QUESTION #324: IT GOES UP IN THE SKY..80
QUESTION #325: IT'S A LONGER PHRASE 80
QUESTION #326: IT'S WHERE THE PARTHENON IS 81
QUESTION #327: THE ANSWER IS IN THE QUESTION 81
QUESTION #328: WHAT A COINCIDENCE 81
QUESTION #329: IT CAN BECOME A CONTAINER..81
QUESTION #330: IT'S PRETTY POPULAR IN AUSTRALIA..81

11

QUESTION #331: YOU SET IT ON FIRE 82
QUESTION #332: IT'S USUALLY GREEN 82
QUESTION #333: IT COVERS YOU 82
QUESTION #334: FLASHLIGHT CEMETERY 82
QUESTION #335: IT'S A VERY FAST DIET 82
QUESTION #336: OFFICIALS OF A SPORT 83
QUESTION #337: NIGHTY NIGHT! 83
QUESTION #338: IT'S A BOOK 83
QUESTION #339: IT'S THE SAME BOOK 83
QUESTION #340: IT'S NOT JUST THE NUMBER OF PEOPLE 83
QUESTION #341: LIGHT HEAVYWEIGHT CHAMPION OF THE WORLD 84
QUESTION #342: CHECK THE PATTERN 84
QUESTION #343: LOOK FOR THE BIGGEST EGO 84
QUESTION #344: IT'S WET 84
QUESTION #345: YOU SHOULDN'T REINVENT IT 84
QUESTION #346: IT CRACKS FIRST BEFORE WALKING 85
QUESTION #347: THEY'RE NOT PEOPLE! 85
QUESTION #348: PETER PAN WOULD DISOWN HER. 85
QUESTION #349: THE OLDEST HUMAN BEING 85
QUESTION #350: IT SLEEPS STANDING UP 85
QUESTION #351: HE PARTED THE RED SEA 86
QUESTION #352: MIGHT AS WELL PLAY ALONE 86
QUESTION #353: THINK OF THEIR BOSS 86
QUESTION #354: AN INTER-PLANETARY FRIEND 86
QUESTION #355: YOUR BELT'S CRIME 86
QUESTION #356: MEANINGFUL NOISE 87
QUESTION #357: IGNORANCE ISN'T BLISS 87
QUESTION #358: IT'S ABOUT SEEING 87
QUESTION #359: NATURALLY FULL 87
QUESTION #360: PARDON THE PUN 87
QUESTION #361: IT'S ABOUT THE GOAL 88
QUESTION #362: ANOTHER BODY PART 88
QUESTION #363: IT'D BE A CRIME IF HE WAS 88
QUESTION #364: THE SAME THING MOMMAS TELL THEIR KIDS AT NIGHT 88
QUESTION #365: ASK AND YOU SHALL RECEIVE 88
QUESTION #366: IT'S ALL ABOUT THE WEATHER 89
QUESTION #367: TAYLOR SWIFT SANG ABOUT THIS 89
QUESTION #368: DELL, HP, LENOVO, ETC. 89

QUESTION #369: OTHER SIDE 89
QUESTION #370: SOME SAY THEY'RE MEANT TO BE BROKEN 89
QUESTION #371: IT'S SPORTS ITEM 90
QUESTION #372: YOU CAN SCRATCH IT, THOUGH 90
QUESTION #373: ADAM LEVINE, BLAKE SHELTON, AND MILEY CYRUS ARE ON IT 90
QUESTION #374: FIRST THINGS FIRST 90
QUESTION #375: YOU HAD MORE 90
QUESTION #376: WHAT YOU SAY, IT SAYS 91
QUESTION #377: MAKES DISHES MORE DELICIOUS 91
QUESTION #378: YOU START A FIRE WITH IT 91
QUESTION #379: INFORMATION TECHNOLOGY 91
QUESTION #380: IT LOOKS EXACTLY LIKE YOU 91
QUESTION #381: IT KEEPS BOATS IN PLACE ON WATER 92
QUESTION #382: ALADDIN'S MAGIC RIDE 92
QUESTION #383: NO NEED TO COMPUTE BECAUSE OF ONE NUMBER 92
QUESTION #384: REVERSE PSYCHOLOGY 92
QUESTION #385: IT RHYMES WITH VOICE 92
QUESTION #386: IT RHYMES WITH FUN 93
QUESTION #387: IT'S SOMETHING THAT LEAVES POCKETS WITH NOTHING 93
QUESTION #388: SPORTY DUDES 93
QUESTION #389: IT RHYMES WITH HICKORY 93
QUESTION #390: IT'S A GAME 93
QUESTION #394: AVOID DOUBLE COUNTING 94
QUESTION #395: IT'S A BOARD GAME 94
QUESTION #396: THE NINJA TURTLES' MASTER 95
QUESTION #397: RARE INDEED! 95
QUESTION #398: THINK OF THE OBVIOUS 95
QUESTION #399: IT'S RELATED TO THE MILITARY 95
QUESTION #400: SKIP A BEAT 95

ANSWERS 96

ANSWERS 1-10 96
ANSWERS 11-20 97
ANSWERS 21-30 98
ANSWERS 31-30 99
ANSWERS 41-50 100
ANSWERS 51-60 101
ANSWERS 61-70 102

ANSWERS 71-80 103
ANSWERS 81-90 104
ANSWERS 91-100 105
ANSWERS 101-110 106
ANSWERS 111-120 107
ANSWERS 121-130 108
ANSWERS 131-140 109
ANSWERS 141-150 110
ANSWERS 151-160 111
ANSWERS 161-170 112
ANSWERS 171-180 113
ANSWERS 181-190 114
ANSWERS 191-200 115
ANSWERS 201-210 116
ANSWERS 211-220 117
ANSWERS 221-230 118
ANSWERS 231-240 119
ANSWERS 241-250 120
ANSWERS 251-260 121
ANSWERS 261-270 122
ANSWERS 271-280 123
ANSWERS 281-290 124
ANSWERS 291-300 125
ANSWERS 301-310 126
ANSWERS 311-320 127
ANSWERS 321-330 128
ANSWERS 331-340 129
ANSWERS 341-350 130
ANSWERS 351-360 131
ANSWERS 361-370 132
ANSWERS 371-380 133
ANSWERS 381-390 134
ANSWERS 391-400 135

CONCLUSION **136**

Introduction

It's been said that questions are signs of an active mind, which is crucial for children growing up to be intelligent, smart, and wise adults. Riddles are one of the best - and fun - ways of stimulating the mind so that it continues to become better and smarter. This book contains 400 fun and smart riddles that can provide very good mental stimulation for you and your kids, and help make your minds develop even more. I hope you enjoy them!

Riddles 1 To 100

Question #1: Whose Son?

A boy had to be brought to a hospital's emergency room. When the emergency room doctor saw him, he exclaimed: "I can't perform the surgery on him - he's my son!" If the doctor wasn't the boy's father, how can it be that the boy was the doctor's son?

Question #2: Time Rider

A cowboy once rode into a small county on Friday. Once there he stayed for 3 days before leaving on Friday. How was the cowboy able to arrive on Friday, stay for 3 days, and still leave the county on Friday?

Question #3: Not As Many As You Think

All throughout the year, how many seconds are there?

Question #4: Kids of All Shapes and Sizes

A grandfather was asked to describe how his grandkids looked like. He said, "All are fat but 2, all are skinny but 2, and all are muscular but 2." How many grandkids does he have?

Question #5: Just Do It

A horse that's tied to a 50-foot chain wants to eat hay that's 20 feet away from him. How can the horse eat the hay?

Question #6: It's All In Your Head

A knife gets duller the more you use it. This thing is the opposite - it gets sharper the more you use it. What is it?

Question #7: International Cabin

A man enters his cabin in Texas. When he exits his cabin, he's in Japan. How did that happen?

Question #8: A Literal Bet

A man made a $20 bet with a new acquaintance, saying "I can write your exact weight even if you don't tell me what it is." The new acquaintance thought this is a sure win because he will just tell the man he's wrong regardless if he's able to write the exact weight or not. The man was able to write it and won the bet despite the new acquaintance's deception scheme. How?

Question #9: As You Were Walking

A man was walking to the mall from his house. Along the way, he greeted 3 grandmothers, spoke to 2 mailmen, high-fived 7 former NFL Super Bowl MVPs, and fist-bumped 10 rappers from the hood. How many people were walking to the mall?

Question #10: Musical Strawberries

A newborn strawberry's crying. Why?

Question #11: Walk This Way

A person is standing on the South Pole of Antarctica facing north. If that person took a step backward, what direction would he or she have traveled?

Question #12: Your Well

A well that's deep and full of knives. What is it?

Question #13: Things Aren't As Tall As They Seem

A window cleaner was cleaning the windows at the 40th floor of a 41-story building when he slipped and fell. After falling, he simply stood up and resumed cleaning the window. How come he didn't get seriously or fatally injured?

Question #14: Legal Violation

A woman who is learning how to drive enters a busy one-way road, looks at the traffic police eye-to-eye, and smiles at him without being apprehended. Why?

Question #15: Breaking the Pattern

A yellow house is made of yellow bricks and a black house is made of black stones. What is a greenhouse made of?

Question #16: A Coat of Colors

All coats are worn dry except for this one, which can only be worn when wet. What coat is this?

Question #17: Unfashionable Dress

All dresses can be worn except this. What kind of dress is this?

Question #18: Violent Ring

All rings are round shaped except for this one that's square shaped. What is it?

Question #19: Super Mario's Room

All rooms have a door except for this one. What kind of room is it?

Question #20: We Are Family

A girl has as many brothers as sisters. However, her brothers only have half a brother for every sister. How many brothers and sisters are there in the girl's family?

Question #21: Cockiest Of Them All

An engineer, an NFL quarterback, and a motorcycle rider enter construction site wearing helmets. Who among the 3 wore the biggest one?

Question #22: Wood in the Wind

As I was walking to school, I saw a man carrying lots of wood that wasn't crooked. The wood he was carrying wasn't crooked either. What type of wood was he carrying?

Question #23: Fast And Furious

As you get near the finish line of a 5-kilometer fun run, you overtake the person who was in second place. What place are you right after doing that?

Question #24: The Love Boat

As you make your way across a bridge, you spot a boat full of people. And yet, there isn't even a single person on that boat. How can that be?

Question #25: Fit To A T

A Turkish national traveled to Tonga just to teach kids to tie their shoelaces. How many letter T's are in that?

Question #26: It's Not What You Think It Is

Bamtaramushkabalurzeekhanz...how do you spell it?

Question #27: It Stays With You

Before going to sleep on your bed, what is the last thing you take off?

Question #28: Pants-Less Barnes and Noble

Besides Winnie the Pooh, what else wears a jacket with no pants?

Question #29: Heavyweight Champion of the World

Between a pound of rocks and a pound of cotton, which weighs heavier?

Question #30: Newton's Football

Brunson kicked a ball all by himself in an open field. It came rushing back to him. How did that happen?

Question #31: Cool As Ice

Compared to what it's made of, it's lighter. More of it is hidden than visible. What is it?

Question #32: Fixed Shades

Despite having tens or hundreds of limbs, it can't even walk. What is it?

Question #33: The Strange Case of Dexter Button

Dexter was 25 years old 2 days ago. Next year, he will be 28 years old. How can this be?

Question #34: Real Steel

Dirk makes shoes with no leather using fire, water, air, and earth. Every customer orders 2 pairs of shoes. Who is Dirk?

Question #35: Wet If You Do, Wet If You Don't

Even if it rains harder, it doesn't become any wetter than when it rained lighter. What is it?

Question #36: A Harmless Stalker

Everybody has this and can't lose this. What is it?

Question #37: All Boxed In

Five people were on their way to a church. When it started to rain, 4 of the 5 ran for cover leaving the 5th one behind. And yet, the 4 who ran for cover got wet as they ran for cover while the man who got left behind stayed dry. How'd that happen?

Question #38: A Different Kind of Math

5 + 6 totals 11. But 6 + 7 totals only 1. Why?

Question #39: Just Between the Two of Us

For one, it's insufficient. For two, it's perfect. For three, it's worthless. What is it?

Question #40: You Can't Wet Something That's...

George dove into the water and as expected, he didn't get his hair wet. How'd that happen?

Question #41: Honorable Coveting

Giving it to someone undeserving is disgusting but taking it for yourself is considered to be honorable. If it were a game, nobody will win. What is it?

Question #42: Olaf

He's a man that's heartless and cold. If you try to give him warmth, he'll slowly die. What is he?

Question #43: Everybody's Here

Hi, I'm Rodney and I live on a farm. With me on the farm are 4 other dogs Brownie, Spottie, Whitey, and Blackie. Who is the fifth dog on the farm?

Question #44: It's How You Read It

How can a book with the title that's read as "how to jog" have nothing to do with running?

Question #45: Air Ball

How can you a ball come back to you after throwing as hard as you can even if there isn't a wall or a floor to bounce it from?

Question #46: The Strange Case of Benjamin Button

How can you be 10 in the year 1880 and only 5 in the year 1885?

Question #47: Combustible Stick

How can you create a fire using only 1 piece of stick?

Question #48: Lucky 1,000

How can you get the number 1,000 by adding only the number 8?

Question #49: A Bat You Are Not

How can you go for 5 days without sleep and feel and act normal?

Question #50: Autobots...Roll Out

How can you make your car not a car?

Question #51: Pirated Coins

How can you tell that a man claiming to have found a coin that was dated 150 B.C. on its face is lying?

Question #52: Long Lost Friends

How did the beach greet the tide as it came in?

Question #53: English Mates

How do you pay dog catchers?

Question #54: Round and Round the Family Goes

How is your mother's sister's brother-in-law related to you?

Question #55: Tea Days

How many days in a week begin with the letter "T"?

Question #56: Not As Many As You Think

How many letters does the Greek alphabet contain?

Question #57: Tickles Countdown

How many tickles can make an octopus laugh?

Question #58: Same as Yours

How much time did a robber get for stealing a calendar?

Question #59: The Answer's Here

How short is this riddle's correct answer?

Question #60: It's a Numbers Game

How would you divide 55 such that one number is equivalent to 1.5 times of the other? What are those numbers?

Question #61: Who's the Fairest Of Us All?

I always tell the truth even if I don't say and hear anything. What am I?

Question #62: There's a Lot of It Here

I am something that ceases to be when you already know and continues to be when you don't know. What am I?

Question #63: Not Meant To Be Broken

I am something that you can make and break even with touching. What am I?

Question #64: Pungency Required

I am something that you release but pretend you didn't. When I'm released, you drive people away. What am I?

Question #65: Crying High in the Sky

I can cry even if I don't have eyes. I can fly even if I don't have wings. What am I?

Question #66: Power You Up

I can die despite not being alive. What am I?

Question #67: Also a Gummy Treat

I can end up either deep in a book or pierced through a hook. What am I?

Question #68: An Equipment

I can enter but can't exit. I have space but have no room of my own. I have keys but possess no locks. What am I?

Question #69: I Raise You Up

I can never go sideways, and I'm stuck in a building that's at least 3 floors high. What am I?

Question #70: Evidence of Approval

I can travel the world just by staying in one spot. What am I?

Question #71: I Won't Tell It to You

I don't have it when I share it and when I don't share it, I keep it. What's that?

Question #72: Not So High

I fell from a 30-foot ladder and didn't get injured. How'd that happen?

Question #73: An Unwelcomed Guest That People Run Over

I go through and around villages, cities, and towns and yet, I never come in. What do you call me?

Question #74: Sweet Dreams

I have a leg, a foot, and 4 legs but am not alive. What am I?

Question #75: Round And Round It goes

I have hands but I can't use them to clap! What am I then?

Question #76: Family Ties

I have no siblings but this particular person's father is my father's son. Who is this person?

Question #77: Colors on the Road

I look at you and you look at me. I can't see despite having 3 eyes. I give you commands by blinking and you obey them by moving your hands and feet. What am I?

Question #78: Command Center

I may not have a tongue, nose, ears, or eyes but I have the ability to taste, smell, hear, and see everything you do. What am I?

Question #79: Pictures Paint A Thousand Words

I neither experience nor own anything but I have so many memories. What am I?

Question #80: Directions

I own waterless rivers, treeless and animal-less forests, and uninhabited cities. What do you call me?

Question #81: Making Melodies

I possess so many keys, none of them open locks. What am I?

Question #82: It's High and Hot

I'm a 4-letter word that is read the same regardless if forward or backward. What word am I?

Question #83: The Correct Incorrect Answer

I'm a word that when you pronounce right becomes wrong and when you pronounce wrong becomes right. What word am I?

Question #84: Records Transactions

I'm a word where there are 3 double letters that follow each other. What word am I?

Question #85: Under the Sea

I'm cold blooded and lives without breath, I'm never thirsty and yet I always drink. What am I?

Question #86: A Shelter

I'm considered both a father and a mother and yet have no child. I hardly stay still and yet, I have never wandered. What am I?

Question #87: You Write On It

I'm dirt when white and clean when black. What am I?

Question #88: I Help You Write

I'm imprisoned in a wooden case after being rescued from a mine and yet, practically everybody can use me. What am I?

Question #89: The Un-Cat

I'm not a cat despite looking, acting, sounding, and smelling like one. What am I?

Question #90: Wisdom in Words

I'm something that everybody in the world would benefit from but unfortunately, most people don't want to take me. What am I?

Question #91: Burn Baby Burn, Burn!

I'm the only thing in the world that will die if given water. What am I?

Question #92: You, Me, and Jesse Dupree

If 3 people can catch 3 fishes in 3 minutes, how many people will it take to catch 1,000 fish in 1,000 minutes?

Question #93: It's a Corrupt Bull

If a bull charges you, what should you do?

Question #94: The Root Determines the Fruit

If a monkey, a squirrel, and a cat race each other to the top of a mango tree, who'd get the banana first?

Question #95: Smoke in Your Mind

If an electricity-powered train is running at 50 miles per hour going east and it encounters a strong winds blowing north, to which direction will the train's smoke drift to?

Question #96: True or False?

If each page of a 600-word book says "Exactly (page number) pages in this book are not true!", is there any page in this book that's telling the truth?

Question #97: A White Flower

If everybody in the United States bought only white colored cars, what would we have?

Question #98: Do As You're Told

If I ask you to say racecar backward, how should you do it?

Question #99: Commander In Chief

If Jerry lives in a pink house, and Maria lives in a red one, who lives in the white house?

Question #100: Aladdin's Magic Ride

If you combine your pet dog with an automobile, what do you get?

Riddles 101 To 200

Question #101: Lean on Me

If you don't want anybody to be able to jump over a pencil, how should you place it on the ground?

Question #102: The Circles of Life

If you draw a circle, how can you make it bigger without erasing and redrawing it?

Question #103: Newline Cinema

If you draw a line, how can you make it longer without having to touch and add to it?

Question #104: Apples...Transformed!

If you have 50 apples and 47 people, how can you share the apples equally among them?

Question #105: Subtraction

If you only have a 5-minute hourglass timer and a 3-minute hourglass timer, how can you make sure that you boil an egg for only 2 minutes?

Question #106: Deeper Inside

If you put a coin in a bottle then plugged the bottle with a cork, how can you get the coin back without having to break the bottle or take the cork out?

Question #107: A Librarian's Favorite Word

If you say it, it ceases to be. What is it?

Question #108: Line and Sinker

If you try to eat this thing, the one who sent it will eventually eat you. What is it?

Question #109: Expect the Unexpected

If you were to be executed and have a choice between being put in 3 rooms, which should room should you choose: the room with tigers that have just finished eating, the room with lions that haven't eaten in 5 years, or the room with a blazing fire?

Question #110: Not As Far As You Think

If your dog ran into the woods, how far can into it can he do so?

Question #111: The Real King of the Animals

Imagine walking into a room where there's a monkey eating bananas, an elephant eating peanuts, and a chow-chow eating dog food. Of all the animals in the room, which is the most intelligent?

Question #112: Pay Attention

Imagine you're a pilot. You're flying a Boeing 747 plane. The plane is carrying 1,000 passengers, 550 of which are female and only 450 are male. Of the 550 females, 150 are little girls and out of the 450 males, 100 are little boys. The flight from Vancouver to New York is estimated to take 5 hours. How old is the pilot?

Question #113: It's Just a Fantasy

Imagine you're in a car that fell of a river. The car's quickly being filled water. What should you do so it'll stop?

Question #114: Christmas Balls

In a bag, there are 60 balls, which is a combination of yellow, green and red balls. If the bag contains as much as 4 times more yellow balls than red, and 6 green balls more than red, how many balls are there per color?

Question #115: Checkmate!

In a battle, there are 30 guys and only 2 ladies. The ladies, however, yield the most power. Each side wears either white or black and can wage war for hours on end. Who are they?

Question #116: Dual Role

In a burger joint, a group of 2 mothers and 2 daughters only ordered 3 burgers. However, each of them enjoyed 1 burger each. How was that possible?

Question #117: The Devil's In the Details

In a circular house, someone spilled coffee on the Dad's white pants. There were 3 suspects, all of whom denied being at fault. The son claimed he was out in the garden playing with the dog. The wife claimed she was out doing groceries. The youngest daughter claimed she was cleaning the corners of the house. Who was the suspect and how did the dad find out who that was?

Question #118: Stairway To Where?

In a pink bungalow (1-story house) lived pink pets (fish and cats). There's also a pink table, pink chair, pink computer, pink phone, pink T.V. - you name it and it was pink! So what color were the house's stairs?

Question #119: It's So Soft

In the morning, it becomes headless. At night, it gets its head back.

Question #120: So Many Bars

In this place, you can finish many books without even finishing a sentence. Where is this place?

Question #121: Hand Reading

Inside a house that has no lights, a woman sits at night. Without any candles, lamps, or bulbs, she is still able to read. How is that possible?

Question #122: A Letter

It appears once every year, twice every week, and never every day. What is it?

Question #123: It Rings A Bell

It asks no questions but it demands to be answered. What is it?

Question #124: The Best Movie Companion

It becomes lighter the bigger it gets and makes a loud sound when its jacket it sheds. What is it?

Question #125: Gone With It

It bites even if it's toothless and cries even if it's voiceless. What is it?

Question #126: Let There Be...

It can occupy an entire room without taking up space. What is it?

Question #127: Borrowed but Not Lent

It can't run yet it has 2 feet. It doesn't have fingers and yet it has arms. It's good with carrying things but it's best able to carry them when its feet are off the ground. What is it?

Question #128: You Lose Track of It Many Times

It consumes everything and doesn't turn back, it only moves forward. What is it?

Question #129: Small But Powerful

It contains all you know but is just a bit bigger than your clenched fist. What is it?

Question #130: Like a Popsicle

It dies in the summer, only to live again in the winter and its roots grow upward. What is it?

Question #131: You Provide It the Head and Arms

It doesn't have a head but it has a neck. It doesn't have hands but it has arms. What is it?

Question #132: Shines So Bright

It goes around your house. It can even get inside it. Yet, it doesn't' touch your house. What is it?

Question #133: Don't Play With It

It grows but isn't alive. It needs air but doesn't have lungs. It doesn't have a mouth but water is fatal to it. What is it?

Question #134: Makes You Look Good

It has 1 entrance and 3 exits. Most of the time, you go out with it. What is it?

Question #135: Filled With Sand

It has 2 bodies that are stuck as one. The stiller it stands, the faster it runs. What is it?

Question #136: A Measuring Device

It has 3 feet and yet, can't walk. What is it?

Question #137: You Wear It

It has 4 fingers and 1 thumb and yet, it's not a living creature. What is it?

Question #138: Gives You Sap

It has a silent bark and doesn't bite. What is it?

Question #139: You Buy With It

It has a tail and a head but no limbs. It can be silver, gold, or brown. What is it?

Question #140: The Lone Ranger

It has a tail, six legs, 2 heads, and 4 eyes. What is it?

Question #141: Nikes, Adidas, and UnderArmour

It has a tongue, can't walk, and gets around very frequently?

Question #142: It Can Also Be a Soup

It has a why but has no answer. It has a bee and yet has no honey. It has a sea and yet has no water. It has an eye and yet can't see. What is it?

Question #143: Creamy and Crispy It Can Be

It has no beginning. It has no end. It also doesn't have a middle. What is it?

Question #144: A Halloween Fixture

It has no eyes but it used to be able to see. It was able to think before but it's now empty and white. What is it?

Question #145: It Has Flights but Not an Airport

It never moves despite going up and down, what is it?

Question #146: Protects From Intruders

It runs around the house and yet, it doesn't move an inch. What is it?

Question #147: Flowing Like a River

It runs smoother than any luxury car. It loves falling more than climbing. What is it?

Question #148: Out Of the Heart the Mouth Does

It shouldn't be judged by its size, it contains truth and lies, it can hurt without touching, it can push without moving. What is it?

Question #149: Bugs Bunny's Favorite Treat

It sounds like a parrot and is color orange. What is it?

Question #150: Pierces Sharply

It still can't see even if it has one eye. What is it?

Question #151: A Kind of Stone

It uses another person's name, makes people cry when they see it, and makes people lie by it all night and all day, every day. What is it?

Question #152: It Contains Liquids

It wears a cap despite having no head. What is it?

Question #153: Make Bread from It

It's a 5-letter word that refers to a type of food. You can transform it into a form of energy by simply removing the first letter. You can change it into something you need to do for survival by removing the first 2 letters. And finally, you can change it into a healthy beverage simply removing the first 2 letters and re-arranging the remaining 3. What is it?

Question #154: A Joke That Isn't Funny

It's a food that you need to remove the outside to cook the inside and once cooked, you eat the outside and throw away the inside. What food is this?

Question #155: It Can Be Scrambled

It's a keyless, lockless, and hingeless box that carries a golden treasure within. What is it?

Question #156: It Was Hidden Under a Princess' Mattress

It's a seed that is composed of 3 letters. Even if you remove 2 of its letters, it will still read and sound the same. What seed is it?

Question #157: See With It

It's a word that can be read or pronounced as a letter, has 3 letters, 2 of which are the same, and can be read the same regardless if spelled forward or backward. What is it?

Question #158: Hardly Present

It's a word that denotes hardly being present and if you take away its start, it turns into an herb. What is it?

Question #159: Always On the Horizon

It's always on the way but will never arrive. What is it?

Question #160: Aquaman's Specialty

It's an action word that reads the same whether read upright, forward, backward, or upside down. What is it?

Question #161: A Plural Word

It's an English word that has 6 letters, which becomes 12 when you remove the last letter. What word is this?

Question #162: Not a Drug

It's an English word that means a great woman, where its first 4 letters refer to a great man, its first 2 letters refer to a male, and its first 3 letters refer to a female. What word is this?

Question #163: Surprising

It's an English word with 9 letters. As you start removing one letter at a time from the word until only 1 letter remains, it continues to be a valid word. What word is this?

Question #164: Classic Volkswagen Car

It's an insect whose first part refers to another insect. What insect is this?

Question #165: Cole Haans, Hush Puppies

It's an object that has an immortal soul, a tongue that can't taste, and eyes that aren't able to see. What is it? Answer:

Question #166: A Totally Black Elephant

It's as big as an elephant - can even be bigger - but is absolutely weightless. What is it?

Question #167: Joaquin Phoenix' Sibling

It's as old as time and still runs despite not going anywhere. It can shout a mighty roar even if it doesn't have a mouth or lungs. What is this?

Question #168: Part of a Convenience Store's Name

It's been said that three's a company, four's a crowd. What are five and six?

Question #169: It Can Be Green and Hot and Comes In a Bag

It's dried only to be wet when used. When it's placed in water longer, it becomes stronger. What is it?

Question #170: Up, Up And Away On My Beautiful...

It's flat in the beginning and becomes really fat when used. When touched with something sharp, it creates a loud sound. What is it?

49

Question #171: A Unit of Measure (Weight)

It's heavy when forward and when backward, it's not. What is it?

Question #172: It's All In Your Mind

It's longer than eternity, its simplicity makes it complicated, it's much wider than life, it can go places without leaving its place, it endangers others without hurting them, and it's able to go to unknown worlds. What is it?

Question #173: It's a Bird That's Not a Bird

It's not alive and yet it has a bird's name, feeds of cargoes from ships, and has a long neck. What is it?

Question #174: Kids in Preschool Sing This

It's one bet you can neither make nor win. What is it?

Question #175: Dumbo Is Best Known For This

It's so close to your eyes and yet, you can't see it. What is it?

Question #176: Full or Half Mast It Stands

It's something that can fly all day without leaving its place. What is it?

Question #177: It's A Creepy Crawly

It's something that can have its back on the ground and yet, 100 feet in the air. What is it?

Question #178: You Can Hypnotize With It

It's something that goes back and forth consistently but not in a straight line. What is it?

Question #179: White and Yellow Is It's Theme

It's something that is beaten and whipped and yet, it never cries or complains. What is it?

Question #180: It's a Part of Your Mind

It's something that is created instantly, can bring the dead back to life, turn back the clock, bring a smile to your face or tears to your eyes. What is it?

Question #181: Eat With It

It's something that many people buy to eat but is never eaten. What is it?

Question #182: It's Also the Name of Courtney Love's Band

It's something that the more you remove, the bigger it becomes. What is it?

Question #183: It's In Your Hands

It's something that you can grow yourself or buy from a store, can be long or short, can be round or square, painted or bare. What is it?

Question #184: It's Half-Meant

It's something that you can play, crack, tell, and make? What is it?

Question #185: You Sleep With It

It's something that's taller without a head on it and shorter with a head on it. What is it?

Question #186: It's Not Hot

It's something you can catch but will never be able to throw away. What is it?

Question #187: Slippery When Wet

It's something you use all over your body and it gets thinner the more it works. What is it?

Question #188: It's a Daily Thing

It's white, black, and is red all over at the same time. What is it?

Question #189: It's Wood You Can Blow

It's wood that you can never, ever saw. What is it?

Question #190: A Big, Bad Wolf Loves This

Its first is thrice in pepperoni but none in lasagna. Its second is in ideas but not in plans. Its last is in Georgia and also in Greece. It's at its best as a whole when it's roasted. What is it?

Question #191: A Healthy Food

Its heart is inside its head and it stands on just one leg. What is it?

Question #192: Sounds Like an Energized Admirer

Make me go round and you'll be cooled but if you do so during winter, you'll be one big fool. What am I?

Question #193: Everybody Is Present

Maria's Mom has 5 daughters: Magdalena, Marietta, Malena, and Maruja. Who is the 5th daughter?

Question #194: Roll Call - Done!

Mark's Mom has 3 sons. One of them is named Brock and the other is named Julio, what is the name of the 3rd son?

Question #195: Something Cheap

Mike was doing renovation work at his store. He went to the hardware store and tells the store owner what he needs. The owner tells him it'll cost $2 per piece and tells him he wants to get 888. He was charged $6 for it. What did he buy from the hardware store?

Question #196: Supply And Demand

No matter how bad things get in Antarctica, people there will never resort to eating gorillas for food even if it means death by famine. Why is that?

Question #197: Hail Caesar Numbers

Normally, XL is larger than L. When is L bigger than XL?

Question #198: All or Nothing

Of all the months in a year, how many of them have 28 days?

Question #199: It's a State

On both sides, it's round. In the middle, it's high. What's this?

Question #200: The Love Month

On what month do you get the least amount of sleep?

Riddles 201 To 300

Question #201: It's a Matter of Geography

One night, a man went out of the house and told his folks that he'll be back as soon as the sun rose. When he got back, he had very long hair and a very bush beard already. Why?

Question #202: Play On Words

One night, a swordsmith, a sorcerer, and a prince went into a tavern to each get a drink. Upon settling the bill, they paid for 4 drinks. Who was the other person who ordered a drink?

Question #203: NBA Teams, One East and One West

Only 2 states have their names in their capital. What are these states?

Question #204: Family Ties

Person A is the father of Person B. However, Person B isn't Person A's son. How can that be?

Question #205: Count It Right

Several journals were on the shelf. One journal is 6th from the left and 10th from the right. How many journals are there?

Question #206: Ravens Are Sensible Creatures

Sitting on a wire were 20 ravens. A hunter shoots and kills 1 of them. How many were left?

Question #207: Flying On a String

Skin and bones yet wide, up, up and away it flies. What is it?

Question #208: It's the Gender

The brother of a painter died and yet the person who died didn't have a brother. How is this possible?

Question #209: In And Out and Final Count

The bus driver takes his bus out of the garage on the way to Michigan. On the first stop, he picks up 20 people. At the 5th stop, 15 get off and 23 get in. At the 9th stop, 27 get off and 8 get on. At the second to the last stop, 9 get off the bus. How many people were left in the bus by the time it got to the last stop in Michigan?

Question #210: Reverse Psychology

The faster you run, the harder it is to catch. The slower you run, the easier it is to catch. What is it?

Question #211: From Under the Sea to Out Of It

The host thinks it's an irritation, but it can't throw it out. Later on, someone takes it out and considers it a treasure. What is it?

Question #212: It's Made Of Paper

The more it dries, the wetter it becomes. What is it?

Question #213: The Side of Evil

The more places it goes to, the less people can see. What is it?

Question #214: It's All About You

There are 10 apples on the table. You took 3 of them. After doing so, how many apples are with you?

Question #215: Oklahoma City Sports Team

I clap without a need for hands. What am I?

Question #216: You Play With Them

There were 4 men in a group. One was the boss of love, one was the boss of gems, one was the boss of really big sticks, and the other one was the boss of shovels. Who were these men?

Question #217: Sky Streakers

These can be bigger than mountains and yet look as small as peas. They can swim forever in a sea without water. What are these?

Question #218: Resting In Peace

This is something that a maker doesn't need, the buyer doesn't use him or herself, and the user never gets to know he or she's using it. What is it?

Question #219: An Oral Expert

This person creates crowns of gold and bridges of silver. Who is this person?

Question #220: It Makes the World a Healthier Place to Live

Though it doesn't eat solid food, it has light meals daily. What is it?

Question #221: A Collectors' Item

Though it doesn't have a wallet, it pays its way going all over the world. And while it does so, it just stays in one corner. What is it?

Question #222: A Hero in a Half Shell

Though it never leaves its house, it is able to row quickly using 4 oars. What is it?

Question #223: It's Possible

Three glasses in a row are filled with orange juice while the next 3 consecutive glasses are empty. How can you arrange the glasses - moving just 1 glass - so that the full and empty glasses alternate?

Question #224: You Light It Up

To extend its life, you have to kill it. What is it?

Question #225: Crossing a River

To open, it closes. To close, it opens. Water surrounds it and yet, it stays dry. What is it?

Question #226: Geography Matters

Two babies were born at exactly the same time and date. However, one's older than the other. How'd that happen?

Question #227: Two's Company, Three's a Crowd

Two boys were born on the same date, same time, and to the same parents. Still, they're not considered twins. Why is that so?

Question #228: Do the Math

Using math symbols in place of the asterisks (*), convert this mathematical question into an equation: 12 * 2 * 7 * 4 = 9

Question #229: Literally

What 2 letters are always in sight but always invisible?

Question #230: Unofficial Days

What 3 consecutive days don't have any of the 7 days of the week?

Question #231: It's a Numbers Game

What 3 numbers, whether added together or multiplied together, reveal the same answer?

Question #232: Lays Golden Eggs

What animal can honk even if it doesn't have horns?

Question #233: Honk-Less Animals

What animals can't honk even if they have horns?

Question #234: A Shy Animal

What animal is white, black, and pink?

Question #235: It's a Letter

What appears twice in a moment, once every minute, and never appears in a thousand years?

Question #236: The Obvious

What are cowhides most often used for?

Question #237: The City That Hardly Sleeps

What are cows' favorite tourist destination?

Question #238: Creatures

What are the 2 types of keys that can't open locks or doors?

Question #239: The Most Obvious Answers

What are the two things you can never, ever eat for breakfast?

Question #240: A Government Institution

What begins with P, ends with E, and contains hundreds, even thousands, of letters?

Question #241: It's Not an Actual Body Part

What body part has a good sense of humor?

Question #242: Jurassic World

What came first in sequence, the chicken or the egg?

Question #243: It's a Song by Rihanna

What can go up a chimney when down but can't when up?

Question #244: Not X-Ray Vision

What can help you see right through walls?

Question #245: It's a Letter

What can you add to the number 1 so it becomes zero?

Question #246: No Need to Dig

What can you see at the center of the Earth?

Question #247: It's a Real Cheese

What cheese is made backwards?

Question #248: You Can Sing In It

What comes down and never goes up?

Question #249: It's A Day!

What day of the week is 2 days prior to the day following the day that's 3 days following the day before Tuesday?

Question #250: Locations

What do an island and the letter "T" have in common?

Question #251: Dual Use

What do the words age, trust, blame, rest, and part have in common?

Question #252: Pay Close Attention to Reading

What do these words have in common: eye, level, madam, and civic?

Question #253: On the Beach

What do tortilla chips normally tell each other?

Question #254: A Very Easy Hunt

What do very lazy dogs enjoy doing for exercise?

Question #255: Aside From a Wet Bear

What do you call a bear that's wet from rain?

Question #256: It's Annoying

What do you call a flying house?

Question #257: It's a Matter of Pronunciation

What do you call a funny book about eggs?

Question #258: Not a Real Ship

What do you call a ship that only has 2 mates and no captain or other crews on board?

Question #259: It's a Container

What do you call a thing that has no head but has a neck?

Question #260: Square Pants

What do you call an object that can hold water despite being riddled with so many holes?

Question #261: She Played a Role in The Beauty and The Beast

What do you call an object that is full of T's: it starts with T, ends with T, and is filled with T?

Question #262: Hydrophobic Rocks

What do you call rocks that you'll never find in the ocean?

Question #263: You Can't Stop It From Going Up

What do you have that never goes down after going up?

Question #264: It's a Food

What do you need to break first before using?

Question #265: Food Related

What English action word can be changed to its past tense simply by rearranging its letters?

Question #266: It Hurts

What English word that is more than 2 letters long that begins with "he" and end with "he" as well?

Question #267: No Need for Deep Thinking Here

What happens to a green rock if you threw it into the Red Sea?

Question #268: You Can Play With It

What has a heart but is cold and emotionless?

Question #269: It's a Wet Bed

What is a bed that no one sleeps on?

Question #270: A Lionel Richie Classic Hit

What is a bubblegum's favorite thing to say to a shoe?

Question #271: Mutant?

What is a man who doesn't have all his fingers on one hand called?

Question #272: Waiting For Your Turn

What is an English word that even if you remove all but 1 letter, it's still read the same?

Question #273: A Body Part

What is better tasting than smelling?

Question #274: A 5-Letter Word

What is considered to be the longest word in the world?

Question #275: It's Always Being Set During Meals

What is it that can't walk despite having 4 legs?

Question #276: Youngsters

What is it that cats have that no other animals on earth can ever have?

Question #277: Sit On It

What is it that despite having 3 legs, can't walk?

Question #278: Hollywood Has Lots of Them

What is it that disappears during the day without anybody stealing or taking them away and appears in the evening even without being called?

Question #279: It's Repetitive

What is it that doesn't have a body but can speak without a mouth, and hear without ears?

Question #280: You Pick It Up Often

What is it that has more rings than you can count without having any fingers?

Question #281: It Rings But Isn't A Phone

What is it that people almost always answers even if no questions were asked?

Question #282: You Play It

What is it that people cut and put on a table but never gets eaten?

Question #283: It Can Come From A Dog But Doesn't

What is it that wraps around a tree but never goes into it?

Question #284: People of the Sea Can Do It

What is something that despite being as light as a feather, an Olympic powerlifter can't hold for a mere 60 seconds?

Question #285: A Song by Rihanna

What is something that goes up whenever it rains?

Question #286: It Makes Up Most of the Earth's Surface

What is something that runs but never walks?

Question #287: A Goo Goo Dolls Hit Song

What is that one thing that you own but is used more by other people compared to you?

Question #288: Hassle-Free and Cheap

What is the best and most natural remedy for dandruff?

Question #289: However You Look At Them...

What is the common characteristic of the numbers 88, 11, and 69?

Question #290: It's Named Partially After Them

What is the favorite month of monkeys?

Question #291: Especially At the Beach

What is the one thing that the more you take, the more you leave behind?

Question #292: A Popular Song by the Beatles

What is the one thing you will never get to see again, guaranteed?

Question #293: It's Often Green and Leafy

What is the only table you can eat?

Question #294: The Answer's Here

What is the only word in the dictionary that's spelled correctly?

Question #295: The Most Obvious Answer Is the Answer

What is this?

Question #296: It Flows

What kind of bank doesn't hold any money whatsoever?

Question #297: It's All About Distance and Fur

What kind of fur do you get when you see a growling tiger?

Question #298: You Give Hi-Fives With It

What kind of tree is part of your body?

Question #299: It's Fast, Really Fast

What kind of vehicle reads the same regardless if spelled forward or backward?

Question #300: It's Not an Official Language

What language can people speak silently?

Riddles 301 To 400

Question #301: It's All About Watches

What makes a jeweler and a jailer different?

Question #302: It's Still About Watches

What makes a jeweler and a jailer similar?

Question #303: Do the Math

What number, when multiplied by 10, is just the same as when multiplied by 7.95?

Question #304: No Need to Do the Math

What numbers between 1 to 100 contain the letter A when spelled out?

Question #305: It's a Lucky Number

What odd number am I that if you take away just one letter, I become even?

Question #306: It's Alive!

What room in the house isn't for ghosts?

Question #307: It's Heavy

What seven-letter word becomes eight when you remove 2 letters from it?

Question #308: You Sing It in Preschool

What single word has all 26 letters?

Question #309: It's a Dairy Product

What snack can an invisible man have?

Question #310: It's a Very Club-ish Sport

What sport begins with a T, contains only 4 letters, and is very popular the world over?

Question #311: You Cover Yourself With It Too

What thing becomes much wetter than ever even as it dries?

Question #312: It's Part of the Rice Cooker

What thing can't you put inside a rice cooker?

Question #313: A Stationary Traveler

What thing goes through cities and towns, and over hills and mountains but does so without moving?

Question #314: You Can Eat This Cup

What type of cup isn't able to hold any water?

Question #315: A Halloween Staple

What type of Jack has a head but no body?

Question #316: It Usually Stinks

What vehicle has 4 or more wheels and flies?

Question #317: Michael Phelps

What verb or action word reads exactly the same regardless if it's read upright or upside down?

Question #318: The Answer's Obvious

What will you find at the end of a rainbow?

Question #319: You Seal It Before Sending

What word has only one letter, which begins and ends with the letter E?

Question #320: It's About the Bread

What would make a hotdog agree to do a movie?

Question #321: If You Read Carefully...

What's a 5-letter word that becomes shorter after adding 2 more letters at the end?

Question #322: It's a Hollow Word

What's a 5-letter word that if even if you take away the first, middle, or last letter (one at a time only) will still sound the same?

Question #323: Another Obvious Answer

What's at the end of a rainbow?

Question #324: It Goes Up In the Sky

What's the favorite mode of transportation of rabbits?

Question #325: It's a Longer Phrase

What's the more logical way of reading the phrase "I right I"?

Question #326: It's Where the Parthenon Is

What's the most slippery place in the world?

Question #327: The Answer Is In the Question

What's the only word in the dictionary that's spelled wrong?

Question #328: What a Coincidence

When did New Year's day and Christmas day fall on the same year?

Question #329: It Can Become a Container

When does a door stop being a door?

Question #330: It's Pretty Popular In Australia

When I sit, I stand. When I walk, I jump. What am I?

Question #331: You Set It On Fire

When I was youngest, I was at my tallest and at my oldest, I was at my shortest. Tell me, what am I?

Question #332: It's Usually Green

When it's alive we bury it in the ground and when it's dead, we dig it out instead. What is it?

Question #333: It Covers You

When it's cold, it becomes blue. When mad, it turns red. And when terrified, it turns pale. What is it?

Question #334: Flashlight Cemetery

When should you bury your flashlights?

Question #335: It's a Very Fast Diet

When should you wear a helmet and a seatbelt to dinner?

Question #336: Officials of a Sport

When you leave home, turn left thrice to return home, and face two masked men as you come home, who are those masked men?

Question #337: Nighty night!

When you're asked this question, you can't honestly answer with a yes. What is it?

Question #338: It's a Book

Where can you find Friday going before Thursday?

Question #339: It's the Same Book

Where does the future come before the past?

Question #340: It's Not Just the Number of People

Which is cheaper: bringing your Mother twice to the same movie or bringing 2 friends once to a movie?

Question #341: Light Heavyweight Champion of the World

Which is heavier, a ton of steel or 2 tons of feathers?

Question #342: Check the Pattern

Which of the following words don't belong: Jail Fail Mail Sail Bail Nail and Hail?

Question #343: Look For the Biggest Ego

Which of the football team's players wears the largest helmet?

Question #344: It's Wet

While I have no legs and can't walk, I can always run. What am I?

Question #345: You Shouldn't Reinvent It

While it always travels straight, it always goes around in circles. No matter where it's led, it doesn't complain.

Question #346: It Cracks First Before Walking

While it doesn't have legs and bones, it will eventually walk around after being kept warm for a period of time.

Question #347: They're Not People!

While two twins are in the room together with a King and Queen, there weren't any adults there. Why?

Question #348: Peter Pan Would Disown Her.

Who is the fairy character that rarely takes a bath, if ever?

Question #349: The Oldest Human Being

Who is the fastest human being who ever lived?

Question #350: It Sleeps Standing Up

Who never takes off shoes even while sleeping?

Question #351: He Parted the Red Sea

Who was the first person who ever used a tablet?

Question #352: Might As Well Play Alone

Why are pigs the worst basketball teammates ever?

Question #353: Think Of Their Boss

Why couldn't the sailors in a ship play cards?

Question #354: An Inter-Planetary Friend

Why did Mickey Mouse decide to become an astronaut?

Question #355: Your Belt's Crime

Why did the cops put your belt in jail?

Question #356: Meaningful Noise

Why do bees buzz all the time?

Question #357: Ignorance Isn't Bliss

Why do lions prefer eating meat that's raw?

Question #358: It's About Seeing

Why do many people find the Mississippi river weird?

Question #359: Naturally Full

Why do your teddy bears never feel hungry, ever?

Question #360: Pardon the Pun

Why is it that dragons sleep during the day?

Question #361: It's About the Goal

Why is it that the things you're looking for and find are always at the last place where you looked?

Question #362: Another Body Part

Why is your nose less than 12 inches long?

Question #363: It'd Be a Crime If He Was

Why shouldn't a man living in the United States be buried in the Philippines?

Question #364: The Same Thing Mommas Tell Their Kids at Night

Why would bees pour honey under their pillows?

Question #365: Ask and You Shall Receive

You are experiencing a near-death experience and your spirit, after traveling a tunnel of light, arrives at a fork. To the left is the door that leads to back to your body and the other door on to the afterlife. Each door has a guard and one of them always tells the truth while the other always lies. What should you ask each so you'd know which door to enter to get back into your body?

Question #366: It's All About the Weather

You are with a group of 5 other people that are going out for burgers but only 1 has an umbrella that's good for just 1 person at a time. All of you were able to get to the burger joint as dry as the desert. How'd that happen?

Question #367: Taylor Swift Sang About This

You can easily get into it but getting out of it can be very difficult. What is it?

Question #368: Dell, HP, Lenovo, Etc.

You can enter but can't come in. It has space but has no room for you. Its keys aren't able to open any doors or locks. What is it?

Question #369: Other Side

You can hold this using your left hand only. What is it?

Question #370: Some Say They're Meant to Be Broken

You can only keep this after you give it to someone else. What is it?

Question #371: It's Sports Item

You can serve it but no one can ever eat it. What is it?

Question #372: You Can Scratch It, Though

You can touch me despite not being able to see me. It can be put out but it can never be put away. What is it?

Question #373: Adam Levine, Blake Shelton, and Miley Cyrus Are On It

You can't see or touch it. However, you can hear it. What is it?

Question #374: First Things First

You enter a dark room with a fireplace, a match, a candle, and a kerosene lamp. Which of the 4 things will you light first?

Question #375: You Had More

You gave your brother as much money as you're starting with. Then, your brother gave you back as much as you had left. Next, you gave your brother as much money as he now has, which left you with no more money and your brother $80. How much did you and your brother have at the start?

Question #376: What You Say, It Says

You heard me several times and you'll hear me again. When I die, just call me and I'll live again. What am I?

Question #377: Makes Dishes More Delicious

You remove my skin from me, it's you who will cry and not I. What am I?

Question #378: You Start a Fire With It

You scratch my head when you take me, and afterward, it turns to black from red. What am I?

Question #379: Information Technology

You see a sign that says "Railroad Crossing - Watch Out For Trains". How do you spell it without using the letter "R"?

Question #380: It Looks Exactly Like You

You see it on water and yet, it somehow stays dry. What is it?

Question #381: It Keeps Boats in Place On Water

You throw me away when you use me, and take me back when you don't. What am I?

Question #382: Aladdin's Magic Ride

You use this by foot but buy it by the yard. What is it?

Question #383: No Need to Compute Because Of One Number

You'll arrive at what number if you multiply all of a telephone keypad's numbers?

Question #384: Reverse Psychology

You're given a 10 meter long wire fencing. With that, how can you use the wire fencing to cover the largest area possible?

Question #385: It Rhymes With Voice

You're given something such that you'll either have 2 of it or none?

Question #386: It Rhymes With Fun

Your friend has 10 or more sons. The same friend has less than 10 sons. The same friend has at least 1 son. If only 1 of these 3 declarations are true, how many sons does your friend have?

Question #387: It's Something That Leaves Pockets With Nothing

Your pants pockets are empty and yet it can still have something. What is that something?

Question #388: Sporty Dudes

Mike has 3 buddies in school. Tom, Gabby, and Paul. Of the 3, 2 play golf, 2 play tennis, and 2 play basketball. The one who doesn't play golf also doesn't play tennis, and the one who doesn't play basketball doesn't play golf. If girls don't play basketball, which sport does each person play?

Question #389: It Rhymes With Hickory

It's always found in the past, can be made now, and can never be ruined by the future. What is it?

Question #390: It's a Game

A man pushes his car on the road. As soon as he arrives at the hotel, he exclaims that he's bankrupt. Why?

Question #391: It's Just Your Imagination

Imagine that you're trapped in a house surrounded by zombies that are trying to barge in. There's a machine gun but it's at the tool shed 20 meters from the house. How can you get out of the situation alive?

Question #392: They Don't Wait For No One

What well-known proverb can you form by rearranging the letters in this sentence: I don't admit women are faint.

Question #393: It Rhymes With None

Your friends want to visit you at home and they're all parched! Friend #1 asks for half a cup of water. Friend #2 asks for a quarter cup of water. Friend #3 asks for 1/8 cup of water, and so on with your other friends. In order to serve all your friends water, how many cups do you need?

Question #394: Avoid Double Counting

Going to the mall, you counted about 50 houses to your left. Coming back home, you counted another 50 houses to your right. How many houses did you get to count?

Question #395: It's a Board Game

After being landed on by a horse that jumped over a castle, a man disappears. How did that happen?

Question #396: The Ninja Turtles' Master

It's something I got while trekking outdoors, but I didn't like it. And when I got it, it was hidden from my sight. The harder I looked for it, the less I liked it. And I eventually took it home in my hand because I never found it. What is it?

Question #397: Rare Indeed!

Why is the number sequence 8549176320 such a rare sequence?

Question #398: Think Of the Obvious

How many letters are there in a paragraph?

Question #399: It's Related To the Military

Where in the world is 1900 + 20 the same as 2000 - 40?

Question #400: Skip A Beat

The 22nd and 24th Presidents of the United States weren't brothers despite being born to the same set of parents. How's this possible?

Answers

Answers 1-10

Answer #1: The emergency room doctor was the boy's mom.

Answer #2: He rode into the county on a horse named Friday.

Answer #3: Every month has a 2nd day!

Answer #4: 3

Answer #5: Just walk towards it. The 50-foot chain isn't tied to anything other than the horse.

Answer #6: Your brain.

Answer #7: He's a pilot and he entered his plane's cabin.

Answer #8: The man wrote "your exact weight", which was what he promised he'll do.

Answer #9: One - you were walking to the mall remember?

Answer #10: Its parents were caught in a jam.

Answers 11-20

Answer #11: North.

Answer #12: Your Mouth

Answer #13: He was cleaning the windows from within the building

Answer #14: Because she wasn't driving at that time - she was walking

Answer #15: Glass

Answer #16: A coat of paint.

Answer #17: An address.

Answer #18: A boxing ring.

Answer #19: A mushroom.

Answer #20: 4 sisters and 3 brothers.

Answers 21-30

Answer #21: The one with the biggest head, of course!

Answer #22: Sawdust.

Answer #23: Second place - you took the place of the person you overtook.

Answer #24: The boat was filled with married people and hence, there were no single people there.

Answer #25: There are only 2 T's in the word ThaT.

Answer #26: I and T ("it").

Answer #27: Your feet. You take them off the floor.

Answer #28: A book.

Answer #29: Neither because they weight the same: 1 pound.

Answer #30: Brunson kicked the ball upward.

Answers 31-30

Answer #31: Iceberg.

Answer #32: A tree.

Answer #33: Today is January 1. Two days ago was December 30, and his 26th birthday was yesterday, December 30. On December 30 this year, he turns 27 and next year, he turns 28 on December 30.

Answer #34: HE'S A BLACKSMITH WHO MAKES HORSESHOES.

Answer #35: Water.

Answer #36: A shadow.

Answer #37: The 5th person was in a coffin and the 4 other people were the pallbearers.

Answer #38: It's a clock.

Answer #39: A secret.

Answer #40: George was bald.

Answers 41-50

Answer #41: Blame.

Answer #42: Snowman.

Answer #43: Me, Rodney.

Answer #44: It's part of an encyclopedia series where the book contains topics starting with the letters HOW up to JOG.

Answer #45: Throw it up as high as you can.

Answer #46: You have to be born in 1890 B.C. (before Christ), where the year progresses backward to zero.

Answer #47: By using a matchstick.

Answer #48: 8 + 888 +8 + 88 + 8 + 8

Answer #49: You sleep in the evenings.

Answer #50: Turn it (take a turn) into a parking lot.

Answers 51-60

Answer #51: B.C. means Before Christ and prior to the birth of Christ, dates weren't conceptualized and used yet. That's why it's impossible for an old coin to be dated 150 B.C. on its face.

Answer #52: Hi! Long time no sea (see)!

Answer #53: By the "pound".

Answer #54: He's your father.

Answer #55: 4: Tuesday, Thursday, Today, and Tomorrow.

Answer #56: 16. The (3) Greek (5) alphabet (8) equals 16 letters.

Answer #57: Ten tickles (tentacles, get it?).

Answer #58: 12 months (there are 12 months in a calendar).

Answer #59: How short.

Answer #60: 22 and 33.

Answers 61-70

Answer #61: A mirror.

Answer #62: A riddle.

Answer #63: A promise.

Answer #64: Your fart.

Answer #65: A cloud.

Answer #66: A battery.

Answer #67: A worm.

Answer #68: A computer keyboard.

Answer #69: An elevator.

Answer #70: A stamp.

Answers 71-80

Answer #71: A secret.

Answer #72: I fell from the first step only.

Answer #73: A street.

Answer #74: A Bed.

Answer #75: A clock.

Answer #76: The son of the person telling the riddle.

Answer #77: Traffic lights.

Answer #78: Your brain.

Answer #79: A photo album.

Answer #80: A map.

Answers 81-90

Answer #81: A piano.

Answer #82: NOON.

Answer #83: Wrong.

Answer #84: Bookkeeper - the double letters O, K, and E follow each other.

Answer #85: A fish.

Answer #86: A tree.

Answer #87: Blackboard.

Answer #88: A pencil's lead.

Answer #89: A kitten.

Answer #90: Advice.

Answers 91-100

Answer #91: A fire.

Answer #92: 3 people. For every minute, 3 people catch 1 fish (3 fishes ÷ 3 minutes = 1 fish per minute). So to catch 500 fish in 500 minutes, 3 people are required.

Answer #93: Pay off the charges!

Answer #94: None! It's a mango tree and not a banana tree. Therefore, no one gets to the banana first.

Answer #95: None. An electric train - compared to the old generation steam train - doesn't produce smoke because it runs on electricity.

Answer #96: Yes, the 599th page is telling the truth because if this page is indeed telling the truth, then the remaining 599 pages (pages 1 to 598 and page 600) aren't telling the truth.

Answer #97: A white carnation (car nation, get it?).

Answer #98: Racecar backward.

Answer #99: The President of the United States of America.

Answer #100: A carpet (car + pet)!

Answers 101-110

Answer #101: Put it beside a wall.

Answer #102: Draw a smaller circle right beside it so it becomes the "bigger" circle.

Answer #103: Draw a shorter line beside it so it becomes the longer line.

Answer #104: Turn apples into apple sauce.

Answer #105: Once your water starts boiling, flip both the 5-minute and 3-minute timers. Once the 3-minute timer's done, it means the 5-minute timer still has 2 minutes left. Put the egg in the boiling water and once the 5-minute timer's done, take the egg out of the boiling water.

Answer #106: Push the cork inside the bottle to clear the bottle's opening.

Answer #107: Silence.

Answer #108: A fish hook.

Answer #109: The room with the lions. If they haven't eaten for 5 years, they're already dead by now. So that's where you'll be safe.

Answer #110: Only half way because beyond that, he'd be running out of the woods already.

Answers 111-120

Answer #111: You! You're a mammal!

Answer #112: As old as you are. Remember, you're the pilot!

Answer #113: Stop imagining.

Answer #114: 36 yellow balls, 9 red balls, and 15 green balls.

Answer #115: Chess pieces.

Answer #116: The group consisted of a grandmother, a mother, and a daughter. The mother is both a daughter of the grandmother and the mother of the daughter so there were 2 mothers and 2 daughters in the group.

Answer #117: The youngest daughter because her alibi doesn't check out: their house had no corners because it was a circular one!

Answer #118: None, because bungalows don't have a 2nd story and hence, no need for stairs.

Answer #119: A pillow.

Answer #120: Prison. You can read as many books as you like without finishing your prison sentence.

Answers 121-130

Answer #121: The woman is blind and she's reading a braille.

Answer #122: The letter "E".

Answer #123: A telephone.

Answer #124: Popcorn.

Answer #125: The wind.

Answer #126: Light.

Answer #127: A wheelbarrow.

Answer #128: Time.

Answer #129: Your brain.

Answer #130: An icicle.

Answers 131-140

Answer #131: A shirt.

Answer #132: The sun.

Answer #133: Fire.

Answer #134: A shirt.

Answer #135: Hourglass.

Answer #136: A yardstick.

Answer #137: A glove.

Answer #138: A tree.

Answer #139: A coin.

Answer #140: A horse with a cowboy riding it.

Answers 141-150

Answer #141: A shoe.

Answer #142: The alphabet. It has a why (y), a bee (b), a sea (c) and an eye (i) in it.

Answer #143: A donut.

Answer #144: A skull.

Answer #145: A flight of stairs.

Answer #146: Fence.

Answer #147: Water.

Answer #148: Words.

Answer #149: Carrot.

Answer #150: A needle.

Answers 151-160

Answer #151: A tombstone.

Answer #152: A bottle.

Answer #153: Wheat. It can become heat, eat, and tea.

Answer #154: A corn on the cob. To cook the inside (kernels), you remove the husk (outside). To eat after cooking, you eat the outside (the kernels) and throw away the cob (the inside).

Answer #155: An egg, which contains a "golden" yolk.

Answer #156: Pea. Take away E and A it still reads and sounds the same.

Answer #157: An EYE.

Answer #158: Sparsley.

Answer #159: Tomorrow.

Answer #160: SWIMS

Answers 161-170

Answer #161: Dozens. Remove S and it becomes dozen, meaning a group of 12.

Answer #162: Heroine

Answer #163: Startling. Removing 1 letter at a time, it becomes, starting, staring, string, sting, sing, sin, in, and finally, I.

Answer #164: A beetle.

Answer #165: A shoe.

Answer #166: An elephant's shadow.

Answer #167: Waterfalls.

Answer #168: Eleven (4 + 5 = 11).

Answer #169: A teabag.

Answer #170: A balloon.

Answers 171-180

Answer #171: A ton, which is "not" in reverse.

Answer #172: The imagination.

Answer #173: A crane.

Answer #174: The alphabet.

Answer #175: Your ears.

Answer #176: A flag.

Answer #177: A centipede.

Answer #178: A pendulum.

Answer #179: An egg.

Answer #180: Memories.

Answers 181-190

Answer #181: Plates.

Answer #182: A hole.

Answer #183: Fingernails.

Answer #184: A joke.

Answer #185: A pillow.

Answer #186: A cold.

Answer #187: Soap bar.

Answer #188: Newspapers, which are printed in black and white and is read all over.

Answer #189: Sawdust.

Answer #190: A pig.

Answers 191-200

Answer #191: A cabbage.

Answer #192: An electric fan.

Answer #193: Maria.

Answer #194: Mark - he's one of the 3 sons because they have the same mom.

Answer #195: A store number sign. 888 has 3 numbers and at $2 each, his bill was $6.

Answer #196: It's because there aren't any gorillas living there.

Answer #197: When it's a Roman numeral.

Answer #198: All of them.

Answer #199: Ohio. It has the letter O, which is rounded, on both sides and in the middle is "hi".

Answer #200: February, because it has the least number of days/nights.

Answers 201-210

Answer #201: He lives in Alaska, where the sun rises after 6 months.

Answer #202: The knight! The term "one night" can also be taken to mean as "one knight" when read out loud. Therefore, there were 4 of them that checked into a tavern and ordered drinks!

Answer #203: Indianapolis and Oklahoma City.

Answer #204: Person B is the daughter of Person A.

Answer #205: 15 Journals

Answer #206: All the others flew upon hearing the gunshot and seeing their pal dead.

Answer #207: A kite.

Answer #208: The painter was a woman.

Answer #209: One - the bus driver.

Answer #210: Your breath.

Answers 211-220

Answer #211: A pearl.

Answer #212: Tissue.

Answer #213: Darkness.

Answer #214: 3 apples because that's how many you took from the table.

Answer #215: Thunder

Answer #216: The 4 kings of a deck of cards.

Answer #217: Asteroids.

Answer #218: A coffin.

Answer #219: A dentist.

Answer #220: A plant.

Answers 221-230

Answer #221: A stamp.

Answer #222: A turtle.

Answer #223: Pour the 2nd orange juice glass into the 2nd empty glass (the 5th glass).

Answer #224: A candle.

Answer #225: A drawbridge.

Answer #226: They were born in different time zones.

Answer #227: It's because they're 2 of 3 babies born as triplets.

Answer #228: $12 \div 2 + 7 - 4 = 9$

Answer #229: Letters I and S are in the word sight and in the word visible (in visible).

Answer #230: Yesterday, today, and tomorrow.

Answers 231-240

Answer #231: 1, 2, and 3.

Answer #232: Geese.

Answer #233: All animals with horns don't honk.

Answer #234: A blushing zebra.

Answer #235: The letter M.

Answer #236: Covering cows.

Answer #237: Moo York.

Answer #238: A donkey and a monkey.

Answer #239: Lunch and dinner.

Answer #240: Post Office

Answers 241-250

Answer #241: The funny bone.

Answer #242: It's the egg because before chickens came the dinosaurs. And dinosaurs come from eggs.

Answer #243: An umbrella.

Answer #244: Windows.

Answer #245: The letter "G" because adding it to "one" makes it "gone".

Answer #246: The letter "r".

Answer #247: Edam (reverse of MADE).

Answer #248: Rain.

Answer #249: Wednesday.

Answer #250: They're both located in the middle of water.

Answers 251-260

Answer #251: They can all be a verb or a noun.

Answer #252: They all read the same whether forward or backward.

Answer #253: Would you like to take a dip?

Answer #254: Chasing parked cars.

Answer #255: A drizzly (grizzly) bear.

Answer #256: A housefly.

Answer #257: A yolk (joke) book.

Answer #258: A relationship.

Answer #259: A bottle.

Answer #260: A sponge.

Answers 261-270

Answer #261: A Teapot.

Answer #262: Dry rocks.

Answer #263: Your age.

Answer #264: An egg.

Answer #265: Eat, which can be rearranged to ate.

Answer #266: There are 2 possible answers. Heartache or headache.

Answer #267: It becomes wet.

Answer #268: A deck of cards.

Answer #269: A riverbed.

Answer #270: I'm stuck on you!

Answers 271-280

Answer #271: A normal man. Nobody has all their fingers on just one hand.

Answer #272: Queue.

Answer #273: The tongue.

Answer #274: Smiles, because is a mile between the first "S" and the last "S".

Answer #275: A table.

Answer #276: Kittens.

Answer #277: A 3-legged stool.

Answer #278: Stars.

Answer #279: An echo.

Answer #280: A telephone.

Answers 281-290

Answer #281: A doorbell.

Answer #282: A pack of cards.

Answer #283: It's bark.

Answer #284: His breath.

Answer #285: An umbrella.

Answer #286: Water.

Answer #287: Your name.

Answer #288: Going bald.

Answer #289: They all read the same if even if you turn them upside down.

Answer #290: Ape-ril (april).

Answers 291-300

Answer #291: Footsteps. It's because the more of it you take, the more footprints you leave behind.

Answer #292: Yesterday.

Answer #293: A vegetable.

Answer #294: The word "correctly".

Answer #295: A question

Answer #296: A river bank.

Answer #297: As fur (far) as you can possibly get!

Answer #298: The Palm.

Answer #299: A racecar! Try spelling it backward.

Answer #300: Body language.

Answers 301-310

Answer #301: The jeweler sells watches while the jailer watches cells.

Answer #302: They both have watches - the jailer "watches" cells and the jeweler sells "watches".

Answer #303: Zero (0).

Answer #304: None.

Answer #305: Seven. Take away the "s" and you'll be left with "even".

Answer #306: The living room.

Answer #307: Weights. If you remove W and S, you're left with "eight".

Answer #308: The Alphabet.

Answer #309: Evaporated milk.

Answer #310: Golf. It starts with a tee.

Answers 311-320

Answer #311: A towel because it sucks up water from your body when you use it to dry yourself.

Answer #312: It's cover. It won't fit.

Answer #313: A road.

Answer #314: A cupcake.

Answer #315: A jack-o-lantern.

Answer #316: A garbage truck.

Answer #317: SWIMS

Answer #318: The end of the rainbow.

Answer #319: Envelope, it starts and ends with "E" and contains just one letter inside.

Answer #320: If the roll (role) is good enough.

Answers 321-330

Answer #321: Short.

Answer #322: Empty.

Answer #323: The letter W.

Answer #324: The hare-plane.

Answer #325: Right between the eyes (I's).

Answer #326: Greece (grease).

Answer #327: The word "wrong".

Answer #328: Every year!

Answer #329: When it's ajar (a jar, get it?)

Answer #330: Kangaroo.

Answers 331-340

Answer #331: A candle.

Answer #332: A plant.

Answer #333: The human skin.

Answer #334: When their batteries have already died.

Answer #335: When you're on a crash diet.

Answer #336: An umpire and a catcher. The home is the home base and you turn left thrice when you go to the 2nd base, 3rd base, and home base.

Answer #337: Are you asleep?

Answer #338: In the dictionary, where words are arranged according to spelling.

Answer #339: In the dictionary.

Answer #340: Bringing 2 friends to a movie once, because you'll only pay for 3 people while bringing your Mom twice to a movie will make you pay for 4 people.

Answers 341-350

Answer #341: The feathers. It's because it's 2 tons compared to only 1 ton of steel.

Answer #342: Or

Answer #343: The player with the largest head, of course!

Answer #344: A river.

Answer #345: A Wheel.

Answer #346: An egg.

Answer #347: All of them are beds.

Answer #348: Stinker (Tinker) Bell.

Answer #349: Adam. It's because he was first person ever of the human race.

Answer #350: A horse.

Answers 351-360

Answer #351: Moses. God gave him tablets of stone on which the 10 commandments were written.

Answer #352: Because they're ball hogs.

Answer #353: Because their captain stood on the deck, which is a play on the term deck-of-cards.

Answer #354: Because he wants to see Pluto.

Answer #355: Because it held up your pants!

Answer #356: It's because they don't know how to talk.

Answer #357: Because they don't know how to cook!

Answer #358: It's because it can't see despite having 4 eyes (I's)!

Answer #359: It's because they're "stuffed" toys.

Answer #360: It's because they love to hunt knights.

Answers 361-370

Answer #361: It's because you stop looking the moment you found what you're looking for. Therefore, where you find things is the last place you looked.

Answer #362: Because if it were, then it would've been a foot.

Answer #363: Because he isn't dead yet - he's still living in the United States!

Answer #364: To make sure they have sweet dreams.

Answer #365: Ask both guards "if I were to ask the other one where is the door that leads back to my body, what would he say?" The truthful guard knows the other will lie and point to the door that leads to the afterlife and as such, he'll point to that door. The lying guard, knowing that the other guard will always tell the truth about which gate will lead back to your body and as such, he'll lie by pointing to the door that leads to the afterlife. Since both will point there, the other door is the door back to your body.

Answer #366: It was sunny outside.
Answer #367: Trouble.
Answer #368: A computer.
Answer #369: Your right hand.
Answer #370: Your word.

Answers 371-380

Answer #371: A tennis ball.

Answer #372: Your back.

Answer #373: Your voice.

Answer #374: The match of course. If you don't, how can you light the other 3 objects?

Answer #375: You had $50 and your brother had $30.

Answer #376: An ECHO.

Answer #377: An onion.

Answer #378: A match stick.

Answer #379: I and T! I asked how you can spell "IT" without using the letter "R", right?

Answer #380: Your reflection.

Answers 381-390

Answer #381: An anchor.

Answer #382: Carpet.

Answer #383: 0.

Answer #384: Put up a fence around you and say that you're standing outside the fence.

Answer #385: A choice. You're either given 2 choices or none at all.

Answer #386: None. If your friend actually has sons, at least two of these will be true. Since only one declaration is true, it means he has no sons.

Answer #387: A hole.

Answer #388: Gabby and Tom play all of the mentioned sports while Paul plays no sport.

Answer #389: History.

Answer #390: Because he was playing a game of Monopoly.

Answers 391-400

Answer #391: Stop imagining.

Answer #392: Time and tide wait for no man.

Answer #393: Just one for serving them one at a time.

Answer #394: Fifty houses because you counted the same houses going back home.

Answer #395: It was a knight piece in a game of chess that jumped over a rook to eat a pawn, bishop, or king.

Answer #396: A splinter.

Answer #397: It's because all numbers from 0 to 9 appear only 1 time and they're arranged in alphabetical order.

Answer #398: 10 because there are 10 letters in "a paragraph".

Answer #399: In a 24-hour clock.

Answer #400: They're one and the same person, only that he served 2 non-consecutive terms.

Conclusion

Thanks for buying this book! I hope you and your kids had a fun and great time answering the riddles! If you want more, then go check out my next book that'll feature more challenging riddles for you and your kids! Until next time, all the best!

Made in the
USA
Middletown, DE